STUDY GUIDE

THE MOST VALUABLE CATCH

Cover design by Sara Young
Cover photo by Andrejs Polivanovs
Cover photo ship by Philip Stephen
Author bio photo by Jean Johnson Portraits

ISBN: 978-1-959095-72-9   1 2 3 4 5 6 7 8 9 10

Printed in the United States of America

STUDY GUIDE

THE MOST VALUABLE CATCH

RISKING IT ALL FOR WHAT MATTERS THE MOST

STEVE JAMISON

AVAIL

CONTENTS

THE MOST VALUABLE CATCH

RISKING IT
ALL FOR WHAT
MATTERS THE
MOST

STEVE JAMISON

LEADERS GUIDE:

PERSONALIZE EACH LESSON

Thank you for leading a group through *The Most Valuable Catch* study guide. Your willingness to lead others through this journey and into the Word of God is a worthy time investment.

Each week you will gather with your group and preview one of the master class videos that correlate with the book. Within this guide are pages that allow note-taking for each video, along with discussion questions to work through with your group.

PREPARATION

As you prepare to teach this material in a group or class, consider these steps:

1) Carefully and thoughtfully read the book before the nine-week session begins. Make notes, highlight key sections, quotes, or stories, and complete the reflective questions at the end of each chapter. This will familiarize you with the entire scope of the content.

2) As you prepare for each week's class or group, reread the corresponding chapter and make additional notes.

3) After reading that chapter in the book, work through the study guide for that corresponding chapter. Answer the questions, and look up the scriptures for that chapter. Make the scriptures come alive. Far too often, we read the Bible like a phone book, with little to no emotion. Paint a vivid picture, provide insights about the context of people's encounters with God, and help those in your class or group sense the emotions of specific Bible characters in each scene.

4) Tailor the amount of content to the time allotted. You won't have time to cover all the questions, so pick the ones that stand out to you! If you have extra time in your session once you have gone

through your selected questions, ask the group if other questions stood out to them. After the first week, ask the participants at the beginning of each session how they applied what God was speaking to them through the book and study guide throughout that week.
5) Add your own stories to personalize the message and add impact.
6) Before and during your preparation, ask God to give you wisdom, clarity, and power. Trust Him to use your group to change people's lives.

FOCUS ON APPLICATION

The questions for each chapter and your encouragement to group members should be authentic. This authenticity will help your group take significant steps to apply the principles they're learning. Please share how you used the principles in particular chapters each week and encourage them with their growth steps!

THREE TYPES OF QUESTIONS

There are three types of questions, limiting, leading, and open-ended. If you have led groups before, you already understand the importance of using open-ended questions to stimulate discussion. This guide incorporates many open-ended questions to facilitate discussion and to grow deeper.

Limiting questions focus on an obvious answer, such as, "What does Jesus call Himself in John 10:11?" These questions don't stimulate reflection or discussion. If you want to use questions like this, follow them with thought-provoking, open questions.

Leading questions require the listener to guess what the leader has in mind, such as, "Why did Jesus use the metaphor of a shepherd in John 10?" The teacher who asks a leading question has a definite answer in mind. Instead of asking this kind of question, you should teach the concept and ask an open-ended question about the point you have made.

Open-ended questions usually don't have right or wrong answers. They stimulate thinking and are far less threatening because the person answering doesn't risk ridicule for being wrong. These questions often begin with "Why do you think . . . ?" or "What are some reasons that . . . ?" or "How would you have felt in that situation?".

LASTING IMPACT

For lasting impact, we encourage you to lead with three actions:

Pray: Cover all you do in prayer. Your preparation, your reading, and your time with your group. Pray over your group throughout the week and at the close of each session.

Guide: Encourage the participants to follow through on their reading and application each week and attend as faithfully as possible. As in all things, you get out of it what you put into it.

Connect: Throughout the week stay connected with your group through email or text messages. Feel free to even stay connected through social media. Follow up regarding any specific prayer requests that are brought to the group during the week.

PARTICIPANTS GUIDE:

To maximize your study experience, each participant needs a copy of *The Most Valuable Catch*, this study guide, and access to the master class videos. The study guide includes nine weeks of discovery questions corresponding with each chapter in the book, making this a practical tool for personal or group discipleship.

At the end of each chapter in the book are questions written within the narrative for you to contemplate and consider. In addition, for each chapter, you'll find a section within this study guide that offers questions designed to stimulate reflection and interactions with your friends, spouse, or small group. Don't hurry through these. You don't get bonus points for speed! Take time to consider them, pray about them, and listen to the Lord, and then, take action.

"DROP IT HERE!"

"I WAS ABSOLUTELY SURE GOD WAS SPEAKING TO ME THROUGH THIS FANTASTIC TURNAROUND. HE WAS USING IT TO BUILD MY FAITH TO TRUST HIS VOICE."

MASTER CLASS NOTES

_____
_____
_____
_____
_____
_____
_____
_____
_____
_____
_____
_____
_____
_____
_____
_____
_____
_____
_____
_____
_____
_____
_____
_____
_____
_____
_____
_____
_____
_____
_____
_____
_____

READING TIME

As you read Chapter 1: "'Drop It Here!'" in *The Most Valuable Catch*, review, reflect on, and respond to the text by answering the following questions.

THINK ABOUT IT:

Chapter one focuses on God's desire to speak into each of our lives. God wants to be the center of our lives, which means communicating with us in meaningful and life-changing ways. His desire is for us to know His voice and to understand how to discern and follow the promptings of the Holy Spirit in our lives.

Read 2 Timothy 3:16-17 and answer the following questions:

All Scripture is God-breathed and is useful for teaching, rebuking, correcting and training in righteousness, so that the servant of God may be thoroughly equipped for every good work. —2 Timothy 3:16-17

Why is it important to know that God speaks to us primarily through the truth of the Scriptures? How does God speak through His Word to your heart?

_____
_____
_____
_____
_____
_____
_____
_____
_____
_____
_____

In chapter one, we find that God speaks in several ways. In addition to His Word, He speaks to us through our time of worship, dreams, visions, impressions, wise counsel, nature, circumstances, and past experiences. These are powerful Biblical methods. How do they point us back to the importance of scripture as the guide to interpreting God's voice?

_____

_____

_____

_____

_____

Steve shared how he experienced a dream but questioned and resisted that prompting. He described how it took prayer, his pastor's preaching, and the voice of a friend to finally convince him he was hearing from God. Has God prompted your heart in a way that made you seek His confirmation in your life? Have you felt God speaking to you, but you resisted?

_____

_____

_____

_____

_____

God's prompts are the hooks that connect us to His heart and purposes. How much are you open to God's prompts on a scale of 0 (not in the least) to 10 (all day, every day)? Explain your answer.

0   1   2   3   4   5   6   7   8   9   10

_____

_____

_____

_____

When you hear someone say, "God is leading" them in some way, are you thrilled or skeptical? When is a measure of skepticism good, right, and reasonable? Where can skepticism hinder God's voice from being heard?

_____

_____

_____

_____

_____

_____

Take time to read 1 Samuel 3:1-10. Samuel needed Eli's guidance to discern when God was speaking. Whom do you know that has developed a sensitivity to God's promptings? What method does God most often use with that person?

_____

_____

_____

_____

_____

All of us can become more attuned to God's promptings. What specific steps can you take to be more sensitive to Him?

_____

_____

_____

_____

_____

_____

The Holy Spirit moves in our lives as we gather for worship and open our hearts to hear from God through the preaching of God's Word. Are you expectant when you come to the House of God? How can you best prepare your heart to hear from God?

_____

_____

_____

_____

_____

Steve shared his story and how God led him on a journey of faith that years later would give him insight into the dream God used first to awaken his heart toward ministry. He stood preaching in Safeco Field (today, T-Mobile Park) and saw people coming forward to receive Christ in a greater way than he could have ever imagined.

Now to him who is able to do immeasurably more than all we ask or imagine, according to his power that is at work within us, to him be glory in the church and in Christ Jesus throughout all generations, forever and ever! Amen.

–Ephesians 3:20-21

Consider the scripture above and answer the following questions:

The Apostle Paul points us to the glory of God and how He can do more than we can imagine. How are you seeking to hear God's voice and discover His dreams in your life?

_____

_____

_____

_____

_____

_____

How have you experienced God impressing His voice upon your heart in worship (personal or corporate) and other moments?

_____

_____

_____

_____

_____

God has a dream for each of you. It will take different forms and unfold differently, but God's plans are good, and they go beyond your expectations.

GRAB YOUR GEAR

I BELIEVE OUR SOVEREIGN LORD HAS CALLED EACH OF US TO REPRESENT HIM TO OUR FALLEN AND BROKEN WORLD, THOSE UNDER OUR ROOFS, AND THOSE ON THE OTHER SIDE OF THE PLANET. WE MAY BE JUST AS RELUCTANT AS JEREMIAH, BUT WE HAVE THE SAME ASSURANCE THAT THE GOD WHO CALLS US WILL EQUIP US AND BE WITH US.

MASTER CLASS NOTES

_____
_____
_____
_____
_____
_____
_____
_____
_____
_____
_____
_____
_____
_____
_____
_____
_____
_____
_____
_____
_____
_____
_____
_____
_____
_____
_____
_____
_____
_____
_____

READING TIME

As you read
Chapter 2:
"Grab Your
Gear" in *The
Most Valuable
Catch*, review,
reflect on,
and respond
to the text by
answering
the following
questions.

THINK ABOUT IT:

Chapter two focuses on how God prepares our lives to be used by Him. A fishing season begins with preparing the boat and the gear, even pulling the boat out of the water to take care of what is under the waterline. God works in our lives, dealing with the hidden but most important area: our heart. God's purpose in our lives is to prepare us to have confidence that we hear His voice and have the courage to step out and minister in His name and anointing.

Describe how God has worked in your heart to prepare you for greater things.

_____
_____
_____
_____
_____
_____
_____

How do you think captains and crew members of a boat feel when preparing for a new season on the water? Do you think they're excited or do you think they dread it?

_____
_____
_____
_____
_____
_____
_____

What motivates them to prepare with excellence?

_____

_____

_____

_____

Read Jeremiah 1:4-19. In this passage, we find the Lord preparing Jeremiah to become a prophet to the nation of Israel. Discuss how God reveals His call upon Jeremiah's life and works to give him the confidence to step into his role and ministry.

What did you take away when you read God saying, "I am watching over you to see my word is fulfilled?"

_____

_____

_____

_____

Share how God has worked in your life to build your confidence that you are hearing His voice.

Read Acts 4:32-37. The Early Church had great needs, and a man named Joseph sensed the Holy Spirit prompting him to sell a piece of property to help meet some of the needs. How do you feel this moment of obedience impacted and changed Joseph's life?

_____

_____

_____

_____

What does his step of faith say about his love and confidence in his leaders, that he would simply lay his gift at their feet?

_____

_____

_____

_____

_____

_____

Discuss your impression of how Joseph's gift impacted the early church and its leaders.

How was changing Joseph's name powerful to you? Why was it so significant?

_____

_____

_____

_____

_____

Discuss your thoughts on how the Holy Spirit used the changing of Barnabas' name to build his confidence that he heard from God.

How do you feel this experience would impact you?

_____

_____

_____

_____

_____

_____

What role do you feel faith and obedience play in our ability to hear God's voice and respond? How can we serve God's church with greater faith and Holy Spirit sensitivity?

_____

_____

_____

_____

_____

_____

_____

Steve shares two stories of faith and obedience in chapter two, one about their time as youth pastors and God speaking about taking a big step of faith to begin a new ministry as an evangelist. The second was praying for a dejected young man whose dreams of playing in the NBA were being crushed. In these moments, simple seeds of faith and obedience opened doors that would change not only their lives but the lives of so many other people.

Discuss ways you have invested in preparation in your life; how have you seen the effort payoff?

Was there ever a time you wish you'd prepared better (for a career, parenting, managing your finances, health, etc.)?

_____

_____

_____

_____

_____

_____

_____

Consider the open doors of relationships that come when we contribute to the people around us. It can be a word of encouragement, a commitment to pray and support them, a compliment about work performance, sharing a professional tip, or stepping in to help when a team member is overloaded. How important is it to be invested in other people's dreams and spiritual journeys?

_____

_____

_____

_____

_____

_____

As you develop sensitivity to the Spirit, you'll sense His nudges and hear His whispers. Don't think you're crazy! Pay attention and take a step of faith.

HEAD FOR DEEPER WATER

THERE IS A TIME WHEN YOU HAVE TO DECIDE IF YOU'RE SATISFIED TO STAY TIED TO THE DOCK . . . OR WILL YOU TAKE THE BOLD STEP OF FAITH TO UNTIE THE BOAT AND HEAD FOR DEEPER WATERS? ARE YOU WILLING TO TAKE ON THE RISK TO SEE GOD DO GREAT THINGS IN YOUR LIFE?

MASTER CLASS NOTES

READING
TIME

As you read
Chapter 3:
"Head for
Deeper Water"
in *The Most
Valuable Catch*,
review, reflect
on, and respond
to the text by
answering
the following
questions.

THINK ABOUT IT:

Chapter three focuses on taking big steps of faith that will allow you to fulfill God's leading and calling upon your life. When God desires to do great things through us, we must be willing to step out in faith (faith is a spiritual word that assumes risk). This is why it is vital to seek God and allow him to develop our confidence that He is speaking into our lives.

Where there is no revelation,
people cast off restraint;
but blessed is the one who
heeds wisdom's instruction.

–Proverbs 29:18

Consider the scripture above and answer the following questions:

Are you willing to take on the risk to see God do great things in your life?

_____

_____

_____

_____

_____

_____

Read the following scriptures and make a list of the genuine risks taken by Ananias and Barnabas:

Acts 9:1-19:   Acts 9:26-30:

Risks taken by Ananias   Risks taken by Barnabas

_____   _____

_____   _____

_____   _____

_____   _____

_____   _____

_____   _____

Would you have been willing to take those risks? Why or why not?

_____

_____

_____

_____

_____

_____

_____

If Ananias and Barnabas had not been willing to risk their lives to bring Saul into a relationship with the Apostles and the church, how different do you believe his life would have been?

_____

_____

_____

_____

_____

_____

_____

Do you believe that we would have ever known the Apostle Paul? How different would the New Testament story be without their steps of faith?

_____

_____

_____

_____

_____

In Chapter three, two stories of faith are shared, one with Brandon and Janelle Kightlinger's step of faith to venture onto public school campuses in South Central Los Angeles. The second story is about the faith of Paul and Chris Emmett as they faced a debilitating disease.

How is faith the same but different in these two different circumstances?

_____

_____

_____

_____

_____

**Discuss how we can find the strength to
head into these deep waters.**

**Read Joshua 1:1-9. Moses has died, and Joshua is now
called to be the new leader. Discuss the keys to God's
protection and provision for Joshua in this passage.**

What is Joshua directed to hold onto to lead the people forward?

_____

_____

_____

_____

_____

_____

_____

How would you feel being placed in this position?

_____

_____

_____

_____

_____

_____

_____

**Discuss the importance of trusting God and facing
the challenge with faith and obedience.**

Have you thought of faith as shielding you from fear and doubt?

_____

_____

_____

_____

_____

_____

How do the examples of Moses, Joshua, David, and Jesus help you understand the true nature of courage?

_____

_____

_____

_____

_____

_____

Read Matthew 26:36-46 and Luke 22:39-46. Jesus was facing his deepest waters in the Garden of Gethsemane. Discuss the anguish and the sources of the pain and distress.

What did it mean in Luke 22:44 that Jesus sweated like great drops of blood?

_____

_____

_____

_____

_____

_____

Read Hebrews 12:1-3. The scripture states that Jesus endured the cross "for the joy set before him." What was Jesus looking toward as he gave himself at the cross?

_____

_____

_____

_____

_____

_____

What is your motivation, or why should you have motivation to take risks to trust God for greater things?

_____

_____

_____

_____

_____

_____

_____

What are some of the "faith hooks" God provides that put steel in our resolve to trust Him?

_____

_____

_____

_____

_____

_____

_____

The fear of failure holds many people back from attempting great things for God. What do you feel are the keys to stepping beyond fear?

_____

_____

_____

_____

_____

_____

_____

Which of the principles of courage at the end of the chapter are natural traits for you? Which ones need some work?

_____

_____

_____

_____

_____

What difference would it make to grow in those areas?

_____

_____

_____

_____

_____

Avoiding risks is a sure roadblock to life's adventures, but foolish risks tell people to be wary of us. We need to develop that beautiful blend of deep security in our identity as God's chosen, forgiven, loved children, and with this firm foundation, launch into deep waters where we'll need faith and courage to tackle the challenges.

CHAPTER 4

ALL HANDS ON DECK

BARNABAS EXEMPLIFIED THIS TYPE OF LEADERSHIP. HIS HUMILITY AND LOVE FOR THE CHURCH OPENED THE DOOR FOR A MULTIPLYING EFFECT AS HE MADE ROOM FOR PAUL TO USE HIS GREAT GIFTS. HE WAS WILLING TO SHARE HIS LEADERSHIP, INFLUENCE, POSSESSIONS, AND LOVE SO THE CHURCH COULD GROW AND CHANGE THE WORLD. WE DON'T SEE THIS BOLD, SELFLESS LEADERSHIP VERY OFTEN TODAY.

MASTER CLASS NOTES

_____

_____

_____

_____

_____

_____

_____

_____

_____

_____

_____

_____

_____

_____

_____

_____

_____

_____

_____

_____

_____

_____

_____

_____

_____

_____

_____

_____

_____

_____

_____

READING TIME

As you read Chapter 4: "All Hands On Deck" in *The Most Valuable Catch*, review, reflect on, and respond to the text by answering the following questions.

THINK ABOUT IT:

In this chapter, we will study one of the most critical issues of our day, restoring the sacred trust of leadership. Today people are losing faith in government, corporate America, our education system, and, too often, church leadership. We will focus on how we can bring renewed confidence and a new partnership between Christian leaders and the body of Christ. We will discuss and learn how restoring the "sacred trust" and emphasizing shared leadership will allow relationships and ministry to flourish.

Leadership is a gift, stewarding that gift is a privileged responsibility for which we will be held accountable.[1]
—JOSEPH M. STOWELL

Leaders without emotional intelligence cannot lead effectively because they cannot connect with the people they are trying to lead. Leaders lacking ethical intelligence will lead their people into a catastrophe. But leaders without convictional intelligence will fail to lead faithfully, and that is a disaster for Christian leaders.[2]

---

1 Joseph M. Stowell, Redefining Leadership: Character-Driven Habits of Effective Leaders (Grand Rapids, MI: Zondervan, 2015).
2 Albert Mohler, The Conviction to Lead: 25 Principles for Leadership That Matters (Baker Books, 2012).

Read 1 Peter 5:1-7. How would you define or describe the "sacred trust" between a leader and the people?

_____

_____

_____

_____

_____

_____

_____

Describe the "two sides" of the sacred trust and what each believer needs to commit themselves to.

_____

_____

_____

_____

_____

_____

_____

How does this call to "sacred trust" challenge your life and ministry?

_____

_____

_____

_____

_____

_____

_____

_____

Read Acts 11:19-26. Barnabas was sent to Antioch to help lead this young church in revival. While he was there, the Holy Spirit prompted him that Paul needed to be there. In addition to the Holy Spirit's prompting, what do you think Barnabas had witnessed in Paul that would cause him to travel over a hundred miles to ask him to come back to Antioch?

_____

_____

_____

_____

_____

What character qualities do you see in Barnabas that allowed him to make room for Paul's gifts and to share leadership with him?

_____

_____

_____

_____

_____

_____

Why are these qualities so rare today?

_____

_____

_____

_____

_____

Steve described a moment when his dad spoke a word of encouragement to an exhausted crew member. His statement gave a surge of strength that allowed the young man to overcome and press through.

Discuss the importance of having leaders who lead with integrity and encouragement.

Read Exodus 18:13-27. Moses is leading the people, and Jethro (his father-in-law) coaches him that he is carrying too much. What struck you about Jethro's insights and how they released a new era of shared leadership?

_____

_____

_____

_____

_____

_____

_____

Discuss how important it is to create space for people to excel in their gifting.

How would your business or ministry benefit from unselfish leadership and the opportunity to raise up leaders?

_____

_____

_____

_____

_____

_____

_____

What do leaders need in order to delegate and entrust leadership to others?

_____

_____

_____

_____

_____

_____

Read Acts 6:1-7. This passage teaches the New Testament aspect of shared leadership, the selection of the first deacons. Discuss what the leadership qualifications were and how this expanded ministry met the needs of the people.

Take time to share how you feel this step empowered the Apostles and furthered the ministry of the early church.

Steve spoke of the importance of having a crew you can depend on. People who will watch over your safety and not quit when things are tough. People who are committed to each other and the success of the crew.

Discuss how important it is to be a part of a healthy church.

How can you be a part of a crew that lives the spiritual principles of the sacred trust and shared leadership?

_____

_____

_____

_____

_____

_____

As a leader or a member of a leadership team, how well have you seen your team create and encourage a sacred trust on a scale of 0 (not at all) to 10 (to the max)? Explain your answer.

0   1   2   3   4   5   6   7   8   9   10

_____

_____

_____

_____

_____

Discuss how you feel a clear discipleship pathway (such as the four-point Eastridge Church pathway described) can help a church communicate it's vision to people and help create easy access to spiritual growth.

What are the core principles of your church?

_____

_____

_____

_____

_____

_____

How do your leaders use them to keep everyone headed in the same direction?

_____

_____

_____

_____

_____

_____

What are some ways your church can improve its leadership pipeline?

_____

_____

_____

_____

_____

_____

All of us are invited and summoned to join the crew of our local church. We may need to adjust our schedules and priorities, but only the things we do in the name of Jesus will last for eternity. If you're not yet part of the crew, jump on board. If you're already on the deck, consider where you can make the most significant impact.

EARN YOUR PLACE WITH THE CREW

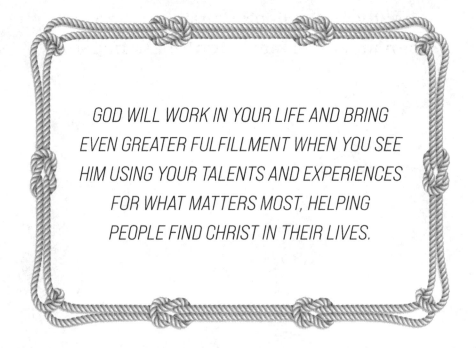

GOD WILL WORK IN YOUR LIFE AND BRING EVEN GREATER FULFILLMENT WHEN YOU SEE HIM USING YOUR TALENTS AND EXPERIENCES FOR WHAT MATTERS MOST, HELPING PEOPLE FIND CHRIST IN THEIR LIVES.

MASTER CLASS NOTES

As you read
Chapter 5:
"Earn Your
Place With The
Crew" in *The
Most Valuable
Catch*, review,
reflect on,
and respond
to the text by
answering
the following
questions.

THINK ABOUT IT:

Our focus in Chapter five centers on how all ministry and business really come down to personal relationships and how we invest in people. Leadership is about creating a positive, faith-filled culture that opens the way for great things to happen. Few things in the church are as important as unity, shared vision, and authentic leaders that people can have confidence in.

Read Romans 12:9-18. Which of the traits Paul mentions is most impressive to you?

_____

_____

_____

_____

_____

_____

_____

How does practicing these character qualities earn a person's place on the church's crew?

_____

_____

_____

_____

_____

_____

_____

_____

What do you think it took for a new crew member to make it on Steve's dad's boat?

_____

_____

_____

_____

_____

_____

_____

Discuss how vital unity, integrity, grit, and a commitment to mutual success were in shaping a great crew.

Do you see these qualities fostered in your business or ministry?

_____

_____

_____

_____

_____

_____

_____

One of the mantras noted from Eastridge Church is, "All quality ministry flows from relationship." Discuss how this is true in every business and ministry.

Share how you feel this statement could help you and your leadership.

Barnabas was a great crew member to have. He understood what it took to build a team and allow others to grow, find meaning, and succeed in their labor. What keys do you see in his life that can be a model for ministry and business today?

_____

_____

_____

_____

_____

_____

In this chapter, the topic of running partners addresses the importance of relationships and the people we run with. We see the example that Steve shares of his friendship with Pastor Jenkins as running partners. Our culture inside and outside of the church is very divided. How can we invest in meaningful relationships that can bridge race relationships?

_____

_____

_____

_____

_____

_____

_____

**Share what you have found as important keys
that help open the door to relationships.**

How important is it to be patient and grace-filled with each other?

_____

_____

_____

_____

_____

Where have you seen people come together and move beyond hurts, pains, or skepticism?

_____

_____

_____

_____

_____

_____

Describe the impact of honoring people and the gifts God has given them.

What blessings are released as we honor one another?

_____

_____

_____

_____

_____

"The ministry of presence" is another key emphasis of Eastridge Church. It centers simply on the belief that we need to be there for people in their places of need. We do not need to have all the answers; we simply come in the name of the Lord.

How has this type of ministry impacted your life, and how can we grow in this area?

_____

_____

_____

_____

_____

Study the following scriptures on the role of the body of Christ. Discuss each section and the importance of the body of Christ operating in a spirit of love and unity together. Share your feelings about what type of crew the church would be if we lived these scriptures to the fullest.

- Romans 12:1-8: Different gifts/roles.
- 1 Corinthians 12:4-30: Distinct parts of the body all working together.
- Ephesians 4:1-16: The whole body working together and coming into maturity.
- Galatians 6:1-5: Restore people gently.
- Ephesians 4:32: Be compassionate.
- 2 Corinthians 1:3-4: Comfort others with the same comfort we receive.

Together, we trust in the leading of God
and the power of the Spirit to accomplish
what He has put in front of us.

SHARKS, ROCKS, AND DRIFT

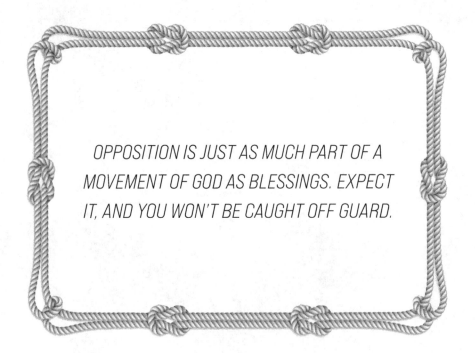

OPPOSITION IS JUST AS MUCH PART OF A MOVEMENT OF GOD AS BLESSINGS. EXPECT IT, AND YOU WON'T BE CAUGHT OFF GUARD.

MASTER CLASS NOTES

_____
_____
_____
_____
_____
_____
_____
_____
_____
_____
_____
_____
_____
_____
_____
_____
_____
_____
_____
_____
_____
_____
_____
_____
_____
_____
_____
_____
_____

READING TIME

As you read Chapter 6: "Sharks, Rocks, and Drift" in *The Most Valuable Catch*, review, reflect on, and respond to the text by answering the following questions.

THINK ABOUT IT:

Sharks, rocks, and drift. This chapter is about our personal walk with God and the decision to live and lead with character and integrity. Too often, talent or charisma has been elevated above the core value of living with a heart dedicated and devoted to God's glory and His honor in our lives. We want to focus on building strength and avoiding the traps of the enemy that has robbed and shipwrecked so many people.

It is simple to understand that the natural instinct of a shark is to attack when there is blood in the water. The shark serves as a visual picture of a spiritual truth about the attacks that will come when we choose to walk with faith and vision.

Read John 10:7-10. What does Jesus say about the enemy and his plans to kill, rob, and destroy? Talk about the difference between the plans Jesus has for us and the enemy's attacks.

_____

_____

_____

_____

_____

_____

Read Acts 14:1-22. This story takes place on the first missionary journey of Paul and Barnabas. Discuss the tremendous ministry that was starting to take place in Lystra.

What brought the change and the attack upon Paul?

_____

_____

_____

_____

_____

What were the spiritual roots of the attack?

_____

_____

_____

_____

Does coming under attack mean they were somehow missing God?

_____

_____

_____

_____

Have there been times in your business, ministry, or your personal life when you have seen the devil try to attack the vision or plans God has put in your heart?

_____

_____

_____

_____

_____

_____

How did you respond to the attacks?

_____

_____

_____

_____

_____

_____

How can we safeguard ourselves from the attacks?

_____

_____

_____

_____

_____

_____

Rocks represent a different type of attack. Rocks represent the temptation to think that the rules don't apply to us. Often, we will try to convince ourselves, while knowing there are rocks below the surface, that we can make it through safely. Sadly, many times people feel that they are entitled or that they can just get away with something they know is not right.

Read 1 John 2:15-17. Discuss what it means to "not love the world or the things of the world."

Too many people reach the top levels of success in business, sports, entertainment, and ministry just to fall off the peak because of moral failures.

What are some of the rocks that are shipwrecking so many lives?

_____

_____

_____

_____

_____

_____

What role do you think pride plays in these failures?

_____

_____

_____

_____

_____

What is the best way to protect yourself and those around you from moral failure and the pain of shipwrecking your family?

_____

_____

_____

_____

_____

_____

Spiritual drift is a dangerous thing to allow in your life. When you neglect the spiritual development in your life, over time you can find yourself far from where you or God would want you to be. This results from allowing yourself to drift without a purpose or a rudder.

Read 2 Corinthians 4:16-18. This scripture speaks of losing heart. Discuss how we are susceptible to drift when we fade away from the church, solid friendships, and a desire to grow in Christ.

Katie Mathew's story of being a passenger with a distracted driver cost her dearly, yet she lives as a triumphant, victorious woman. How can we protect ourselves from drift and also be supportive of others whom we see are drifting?

_____

_____

_____

_____

Great leaders have faced tremendous attacks from the enemy. Attacks do not mean you are out of the will of God; in fact, they may mean that you are breaking new ground and advancing in such a way that you are damaging the kingdom of darkness.

For though we live in the world, we do not wage war as the world does. The weapons we fight with are not the weapons of the world. On the contrary, they have divine power to demolish strongholds. We demolish arguments and every pretension that sets itself up against the knowledge of God, and we take captive every thought and make it obedient to Christ.

–2 Corinthians 10:3-5

Consider the scripture above and answer the following questions:

Describe specific ways the devil uses the strategies of temptation, deception, and accusation. Which of these does he use on you most often? How do you respond?

_____

_____

_____

_____

_____

_____

What are some early signs of drift? What are some later signs?

_____

_____

_____

_____

_____

_____

What are some reasons it's wise to make corrections early?

_____

_____

_____

_____

_____

_____

What is the Holy Spirit's role in helping us anticipate and respond to the threats of sharks, rocks, and drift?

_____

_____

_____

_____

_____

_____

The story of George Reece from the book tells how he was standing for God's honor in his life and willing to give up a promotion and financial gain for the sake of his integrity. What lessons do you see in this example?

_____

_____

_____

_____

_____

_____

As you read this chapter, what is one step of preparation or change that came to mind? What's your plan to implement it?

_____

_____

_____

_____

_____

The Holy Spirit longs to illuminate God's Word and prompt us with whispers and nudges. As we've seen, these are the hooks that connect us with God. We sharpen those hooks by obeying when He prompts us and dull them when we resist.

STORMS ON THE SEA

I DIDN'T REALIZE IT AT THE TIME, BUT GOD WAS FORGING SOMETHING IN ME THAT WOULD SHAPE MY LEADERSHIP FOR THE REST OF MY LIFE. HE WAS TEACHING ME THE IMPORTANCE OF NOT GIVING UP BECAUSE THINGS SEEM IMPOSSIBLE OR BECAUSE THEY'RE PAINFUL. IT WOULD BE A FEW YEARS LATER, WHEN LEADING CITYWIDE JAMMIN' OUTREACHES, THAT I WOULD FACE CHALLENGES EVEN GREATER THAN THE PAIN AND MISERY OF ALASKA. CHERYL AND I HAVE ALSO LEARNED THAT IN PASTORING A CHURCH AND HELPING BUILD A GREATER FUTURE, WE WOULD NEED A TENACIOUS FAITH.

MASTER CLASS NOTES

READING TIME

As you read Chapter 7: "Storms on the Sea" in *The Most Valuable Catch*, review, reflect on, and respond to the text by answering the following questions.

THINK ABOUT IT:

We will undoubtedly encounter storms on the sea as we pursue the future and calling God has bestowed upon us. The presence of these storms should not deter us. We must learn how to respond faithfully and effectively to continue moving on in the face of a storm. What storm are you going through today? What do you believe God is trying to teach you through this storm?

Read Acts 15:30-41. This scene occurs after the Jerusalem Council, a monumental victory for God's grace as the sole means of salvation, but soon a storm would arrive. How do you explain Paul's insistence that John Mark wasn't reliable?

_____

_____

_____

_____

_____

_____

How do you explain Barnabas's continued faith in his young cousin?

_____

_____

_____

_____

_____

_____

_____

How do you see Barnabas' character reflected in his choice to support John Mark when Paul refused to let him join the team?

_____

_____

_____

_____

_____

_____

_____

_____

What do you think it meant to Paul to see the back of Barnabas' head as he walked away?

_____

_____

_____

_____

_____

_____

_____

_____

But now Barnabas is standing with the same resolve as he demonstrated in his relationship with Paul, but this time, he gave the benefit of the doubt on behalf of John Mark. This moment makes me stop and reflect on how deep this encounter was. I'm struck that, at this moment, Paul was unwilling to take a chance on John Mark. It doesn't say the Holy Spirit prompted him or impressed upon him that it would be a mistake. It just says he wouldn't consider it.

Whom do you know whose faith in stormy times gives them extraordinary perseverance? What specific lessons can you learn from that person (or those people)?

_____

_____

_____

_____

_____

This chapter tells the story of the smoldering pit of 911 and the prompt Steve felt to secure Madison Square Garden for a year from that date. How does this story impact your faith to stand in difficult moments to see God's will be done?

_____

_____

_____

_____

_____

Discuss how you would have responded when the check from Madison Square Garden kept coming back.

Have you faced issues like this in your life?

_____

_____

_____

_____

_____

What steps have you taken to trust God in difficult places?

_____

_____

_____

_____

_____

_____

_____

_____

Scriptures give us tremendous insight into the leadership and empowerment the Holy Spirit will provide us with as we seek him. Read John 14:15-27 and John 16:12-15 and list what Jesus said the Holy Spirit would do in the lives of his followers.

_____

_____

_____

_____

_____

_____

_____

_____

**Discuss what it means to you that Jesus called
the Holy Spirit the Spirit of truth.**

Jesus speaks of the Holy Spirit leading us into all truth. Discuss the impact of being able to rely on the Holy Spirit to lead us in times and places where we may not know how to respond.

In this chapter, Steve Jamison shared a day when he suffered a medical emergency that threatened to change his life, his family, and even their church. How has God worked in your life, even through circumstances that seemed dangerous and threatening?

_____

_____

_____

_____

_____

Chapter seven features some tremendous stories of people who faced storms and, with God's help, were led by the Holy Spirit to God's grace and overcoming power. Take time to discuss the stories of Luke and Kate Ridnour standing in faith on behalf of their family, Karen Wright and Bob Mortimer, as they faced potentially fatal injuries.

Life is full of storms. How will you take active steps now to prepare for them?

_____

_____

_____

_____

_____

So, Barnabas walked away with John Mark. I see this as Barnabas living out his convictions as an encourager, no matter who needed his support. In this case, he was unwilling to abandon John Mark because of his mistake. We don't hear anything about what happened to them after they left Paul and Silas, but we can assume that Barnabas protected him from becoming a disgruntled leader, never to be heard of again. Barnabas committed himself to John Mark's success even in the storm. This won't be the last we hear of John Mark.

God used even this moment of disagreement between leaders for good. Instead of one set of missionaries, there were two.

BAIT IN THE WATER

A GENEROUS HEART DOESN'T DEPEND ON TEMPERAMENT, AGE, FINANCIAL STATUS, OR ANY OTHER EXTERNAL METRIC. IT'S ALL ABOUT RESPONDING TO GOD'S GRACIOUS GIFTS TO US.

MASTER CLASS NOTES

_____

_____

_____

_____

_____

_____

_____

_____

_____

_____

_____

_____

_____

_____

_____

_____

_____

_____

_____

_____

_____

_____

_____

_____

_____

_____

_____

_____

_____

_____

_____

_____

READING TIME

As you read Chapter 8: "Bait in the Water" in *The Most Valuable Catch*, review, reflect on, and respond to the text by answering the following questions.

THINK ABOUT IT:

This chapter is about discovering God's most significant keys to a life of meaning, fulfillment, and kingdom impact. How can we learn to sow the seeds that turn empty hooks strung for miles without any harvest into hooks baited in a way that brings back an eternal harvest in our lives, businesses, and the church?

One of the most critical lessons in this chapter is that God loves us and shares the secrets of a fulfilled life. He desires to pull our hearts to himself. One of the key ways He does this is teaching us to love and honor Him through a life of faith and worship.

God desires to be at the center of your life. He has shown us many forms of worship, but the highest form may be honoring God with our tithe and offerings. The moment you read this, a spiritual battle may break out. I want to take a few moments to explain why God has chosen throughout the Bible to teach us the importance of honoring Him through giving.

Read Malachi 1:6-14. The Lord confronts the priests for defiling His honor by bringing useless sacrifices of diseased animals. Discuss why these offerings are useless to God.

Read Malachi 3:1–12. When we give from a heart of worship, we are expressing gratitude, honor, faith, obedience, trust, and love for God and His people. In this one act of honoring God through generosity, it is incredible what it communicates to God about our heart and love for Him.

In the text above, God makes promises about how He will bless the heart that shows Him love and honor. Discuss how important this perspective on tithing is as an expression of love that changes everything.

Have you considered how this text brings a promise that God will let us enjoy the work of our hands and keep us from being robbed of what we have worked so hard for? Discuss the freedom and peace of mind that comes from a genuine relationship with God.

What would it mean for you to "test" God's ability to bless your generosity? Be specific.

_____

_____

_____

_____

_____

Steve shared about his dad teaching him about tithing at sea in a very real and practical way. Discuss how someone in your life helped you learn and understand the role of worship and how giving honors God.

One of this chapter's great stories and teaching points centers on Pete, a friend of Steve's dad, sharing his greatest fishing secret with him. This one tip helped bring greater financial strength and blessing to the Jamisons. God desires to reveal to us the greatest "secret" of how to live in a relationship with Him, develop a kingdom heart, and a mindset that opens the path of true meaning and purpose in all we do.

Read 2 Corinthians 9:6-15. The scripture says God loves a cheerful giver; discuss what a cheerful heart communicates to God. Capturing the essence of this scripture coupled with the teaching and promises of Malachi can truly change your life.

This passage also reveals that God will provide our needs, both bread to eat and seed to sow. Discuss the impact of this passage. Have you been guilty of eating both the bread and the seed?

This text also states that God will provide what we need to be generous on every occasion and that the result will be a harvest of righteousness that brings glory to God. Discuss how this important teaching can change how we view sowing and reaping.

Notice that God gives us two things: seed to sow and bread to eat. The bread is for sustenance now; the seed is sown for a harvest that will sustain us later. Far too many believers look for today's bread, but they don't invest in planting seeds for tomorrow. The result of sowing generously is that the harvest will give us even more seed to plant in the next season, enlarging the harvest. Notice that the harvest isn't just tangible; it's the harvest of righteousness—a greater love for God, more involvement in His Kingdom, and a greater joy in seeing Him use us in the lives of others.

The earth is the LORD's, and everything in it,
the world, and all who live in it;
for he found it on the seas
and established it on the waters.

–Psalm 24:1-2

Consider the scripture above and answer the following questions:

Knowing that it comes from the Lord, do you make an effort to be a good steward of what you have? How?

_____

_____

_____

_____

_____

Many people struggle with feeling that their work is not meaningful or fulfilling. We often look at our lives through the lens of giving God our time, talent, and treasure. Steve has shown us that there is a fourth T that brings all of these others together. It is our testimony, in other words, living with an awareness that God desires to use our lives to share Christ with others.

Discuss the three aspects of an effective testimony. Have you taken time to think through and plan how to best share what Christ has done in your life?

Discuss the concept of praying each day for opportunities to share hope with people.

Read Acts 16:6–10. The Macedonian call was a vital moment of the Holy Spirit prompting and leading Paul. In this fairly long process of being convinced by the Spirit that God wanted them to travel to Europe (first, Macedonia) to share the gospel, do you imagine Paul wrestled with any confusion about what God was up to?

Discuss how God has a way of leading us to divine appointments and impressing his direction upon us. Have you had an experience where God impressed upon you a step of sowing into someone else's miracle or blessing?

**Discuss the impact that reading the story of the
Cuban pastor had upon you. Discuss the blessings
that are often on the other side of obedience.**

What is your risk tolerance in giving your time, talents, treasure,
and testimony?

_____

_____

_____

_____

_____

_____

Think about the story of the Davis family taking in the
Donaldson's and the kingdom's impact beyond imagination. How
does this story challenge you and help you consider investing in
other people and even their pain?

_____

_____

_____

_____

_____

_____

A lot of people have it backward: they think God demands that they give, and they feel resistant to giving in to these demands. It's just the opposite: God has already poured out His heart, love, forgiveness, and blessings on us.. The more we're amazed at His generosity, the more we'll see that partnering with Him through our giving is one of the greatest privileges of our lives.

CHAPTER 9

LEGACY: PRESERVING THE CATCH

GRACE IS GREATER THAN ANY BROKEN PLACE, AND A NEW LEGACY OF FAITH CAN START WITH YOU!

MASTER CLASS NOTES

THINK ABOUT IT:

This chapter brings the whole book together as we focus on legacy and the impact of what you invest in others.

Read Deuteronomy 6:4-9. What stands out to you from this passage regarding leading your family and helping build healthy children?

_____

_____

_____

_____

_____

_____

_____

Read Ephesians 6:1-4. Steve's dad modeled how to invest in the moments of life with your kids—planting spiritual priorities through the combination of words and how they watch you live out your faith. For those who are parents, discuss how you might plant spiritual priorities in your children's lives. The spiritual principles are the same outside of the family. Discuss who in your life you may mentor or have a place of spiritual impact.

Read Psalm 78:1-8. How are you investing in and teaching the next generation? In this process, discuss some of your victories and challenges.

Study Proverbs 20:7. What do you draw from this verse? How can you turn it into a practical action step?

_____

_____

_____

_____

_____

_____

Legacy is not in what you accumulate, but in what you invest.

Barnabas' impact and faithfulness helped shape the Apostle Paul into the leader we know and love. Barnabas' consistent faith opened doors for both Paul and John Mark. This same faith, love, and dedication invested by Barnabas gave each of them the seeds they would need to fulfill their God-given destiny.

Study the following passages and note how Paul invested in Timothy and Titus. Discuss the methods in which Paul invested in young leaders and how he gave them responsibilities that stretched them and prepared them to take the leadership baton of the early church.

Read Titus 1:1-2:15. Paul describes Titus as his true son in the faith. Describe and discuss the leadership authority that Paul entrusts to Titus.

_____

_____

_____

_____

_____

_____

What expectations did Paul express to Titus as he appointed him to build the church and it's leaders?

_____

_____

_____

_____

_____

What is the most challenging task Titus was called to fulfill?

_____

_____

_____

_____

_____

Study 2 Timothy 1:1-7. As you look at this text, describe what Paul saw as Timothy's spiritual foundation and legacy.

_____

_____

_____

_____

Paul reminds Timothy of critical moments of faith that he must reflect upon as he leads. Describe what those moments are and why they would be so important.

_____

_____

_____

_____

Paul was the crucial mentor and influence in the life of Timothy. Read 2 Timothy 3:10-4:8. As you study this text, describe and discuss what Paul wanted Timothy to remember about their time together. When Paul calls Timothy to preach and lead, discuss what that calling entailed. What was the most important aspect of the calling and why?

_____

_____

_____

_____

_____

John Mark would grow into a trusted spiritual leader working alongside the Apostle Peter. He would write the book of Mark, which is believed to be the first Gospel written. What stands out most about the leadership investment Barnabas made into the life of John Mark?

_____

_____

_____

_____

_____

_____

What does it say to you that Barnabas would not let John Mark go away wounded and rejected?

_____

_____

_____

_____

_____

_____

Do you think John Mark would have achieved this level of influence in the church if Barnabas had chosen to leave him behind and travel with his dear friend Paul?

_____

_____

_____

_____

_____

We do not know the inside story of Paul's interaction with John Mark following his refusal to take him on the second missionary journey. Read 2 Timothy 4:11. In this text, Paul knows his days on the Earth are ending, and he asks Timothy to bring John Mark to him.

Discuss what you take away from this statement and the work that God had done in their lives.

King David reveals the pain he experienced in his family from being overlooked. Read Psalm 27:7-11. What can we learn from this story both as people who have been injured and those who have caused the family pain?

_____

_____

_____

_____

_____

Legacy begins with you; it begins now.

What do you think about Allan Houston's story and legacy discussed in the book? How does this motivate you in your journey of building a legacy?

_____

_____

_____

_____

_____

_____

What advantages do people have when comparing God's character with their parents' love, wisdom, and strength?

_____

_____

_____

_____

_____

_____

Like King David drawing the contrast between his parents and God, what are some struggles people with complex family relationships have in conceptualizing (and believing) that God is loving and consistent?

_____

_____

_____

_____

_____

_____

_____

If you left this world today, what legacy would you leave behind? Be specific. Go further in this thought and describe the legacy you want to leave those you love. How much gap is there between the two?

_____

_____

_____

_____

_____

What is the most important concept you've gleaned from this book? How will you apply it? What difference will it make?

_____

_____

_____

_____

_____

It's our task and our calling as Christians to create an environment where everyone—those from solid backgrounds and those from shattered homes—can find their true identity as children of the King. Each one deeply loved, completely forgiven, totally accepted, and called to a purpose far more significant than themselves.

We simply can't afford to mess that up. So listen for the Holy Spirit's prompts and reach for the most valuable catch.

CPSIA information can be obtained
at www.ICGtesting.com
Printed in the USA
LVHW051359170623
750034LV00007B/13